D0871444

INDIA

TIGERS

INDIA
TIGERS

Dianne Kornberg

WILLIAM, JAMES & CO.

Sherwood, Oregon USA

Dianne Kornberg's India Tigers
by Clint Willour

BEING HOSPITALIZED for surgery is unusual inspiration for authoring an introduction to a book of Zen-like portraits of insects from India, but that's what it was for me. Being a captive audience to a plethora of television marathons of episodes of virtually every CI, CSI, and NCIS series, I became aware of a certain communal obsession with the gathering of evidence, which led me to an even greater appreciation for the work of an artist like Dianne Kornberg, who has been doing just that for nearly twenty years.

For Dianne—who began by photographing anatomical specimens before moving on to biological, botanical, animal, insect, and marine specimens—the packaging and labeling of the object/subject is evidence of the care put into conserving these specimens. These photographs show the object/subject and the packaging itself in equal light. Dianne's challenge is in finding unique and imaginative ways of combining those elements.

Which leads us to the photographs at hand—the *India Tigers*. These moths, butterflies, and dragonflies were each carefully folded into triangular packages by unknown lepidopterists in India and then just as carefully unfolded and positioned by Kornberg in her studio. She methodically placed each package at the same position in the picture plane so that they rotate around a central point when viewed in sequence. Each packet is unfolded so that the unfurled sides suggest the movement of wings.

There is another aspect of the paper wrappings. For me they recall both the paper airplanes I made from sheets of paper as a boy and the origami folded papers of Japan. Are we to think of the wings of a crane, that staple of origami? And the airplane reference is particularly apt, for not only does it naturally remind us of wings, but some aviation buffs could make the connection to a plane manufactured by de Havilland named the Tiger Moth, flown by the Royal Indian Air Force from the 1930s through the 1950s.

Kornberg has treated each of the twenty-four images in a very different way. In *India Tiger 1* she positions the dragonfly so that we can clearly read the reference to New Delhi and, through the transparency of the wing, learn that this insect may just be about to take off on official business. *India Tiger 2* makes a connection between the almost yin-yang pattern of the wing and the wonderful writing on the paper. *India Tiger 3*, along with *India Tiger 8*, suggests air mail, with wings and the mail emphasized equally. As further evidence of a harmonious relationship between specimen and setting, *India Tiger 6* works like a beautiful visual poem as the butterfly approaches the word "LEAF" followed by an illustration of a leaf. There is a magical interplay between the markings of *India Tiger 9* and the stains and detritus on the graph paper envelope. I, of course, love the reference to the curator and professor in India *Tiger 10*. In both *13* and *14* we have the contrast between the Ben-day dots of a Roy Lichtenstein painting and the stark whiteness of the insect, with *13* slipping just off the paper as if sliding down a ramp.

Tiger 15 reminds us that disease may have claimed its life, while *17* plays the intricate cross-hatch qualities of the dragonfly wings against the calligraphy of the writing. *Tiger 20* poses a deadly mating ritual between moth and image. In *23* there is the juxtaposition of the "good" purity of the white butterfly and the word "Bad" scribbled out on the paper.

Throughout there is marvelous play of shadow and light moving the objects in a dance across the pages. There is also an amazing sense of volume in the way the paper leaps off the sheet at us, particularly in *India Tiger 24*.

Kornberg began printing her *India Tiger* series as 11 x 14–inch selenium-toned gelatin silver photographs in 1995. Initially she made a series of twelve images. For this book she has produced another twelve images and replaced four of the original series. She presents the new series of twenty-four *India Tigers* as a digital edition. What a delight it is for us all that this inventive and creative artist made the bold decision to revisit a body of work thirteen years old and expand and improve upon the concept.

The Photographs

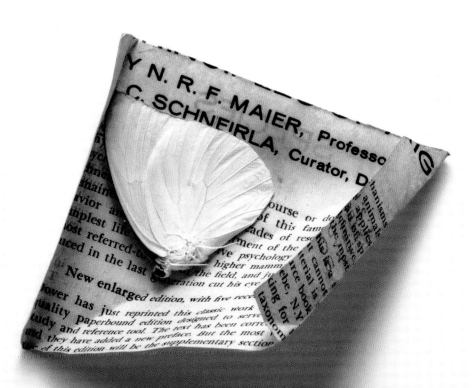

Dianne's Infinite Fugue
by Kim Stafford

A TEACHER OFFERS a box of specimens to a student: Study these . . . list their similarities . . . weigh their differences . . . describe, query, catalog. She accepts it carefully . . . a cigar box labeled "India Tigers." In hand, it seems to have no mass, is buoyant, has lift. She takes it home to an obscure room, a place with good light, stillness, no interruption. The lid of the box is a door, a shutter hinged, aperture to secrets.

Inside, she finds an enchanted series of folded palaces awaiting the sesame touch of her vision. Tweezers to open, a glass to magnify, a camera with which to caress what is there: the winged debris of creation in papers of official business. For the box, it turns out, does not hold entomology, exactly, but, to her eye, it holds elegant wafers of light, small dusty paintings hinged for awe. The teacher has offered her a collection of small teachers, each calling to her most intimate attention. Is this homework, or the early thread of long vocation?

Reading mysteries: The tiger moth possesses a tymbal organ that produces ultrasonic sound to call a mate or deter a predator. The student sees in the patterns of these wings a hint for musical array, a fugue of pivot and hover, a scale that does not climb or descend but spirals, a dance with light. The student can't stop seeing varieties of belief that transcend the family Arctiidae.

Tigers? Yes, there is something fierce in the way these wings rivet illumination, a kind of x-ray fact on the dusty surface of each plane, each wing's beauty oblique from what can be claimed in scientific terms. Spots, whorls, concentric perimeters read not as simple taxonomic clues but as code for the visual apprehensions that tutored Sanskrit. And the bindles of paper hold creation's secrets: the news, notes, scrawls of human commerce opening to reveal the sacred.

Someone's fingers creased these paper scraps to preserve the specimens. See how cleverly the paper is folded like wings, then kinked to close and hold. Notice on these scraps random clues of print and script, chance calligraphy fragmented from another world. Wonder what it would take to stitch back together the meadow where these creatures dwelt, the summer when this collector rambled, the moment when the net cut away the small life from its matrix of wild change, and the evening work of folding little cocoons of paper to send these specimens away.

Tiger moth, dragonfly, damselfly—tiger, dragon, girl. Here each winged episode of seeing could be a book two pages long, read by the hungry eye. Twenty-four tigers are a library for the apprehension of a lost language: six soft feet settling on the upheld finger of a child in the miniature infinity of a parent's momentary disregard.

In Dianne's infinite fugue of light and shadow, we look closely at holy things, as if reading scripture on paper so thin it could be troubled by breath. These photographs hold arresting layers of semi-transparent truth: the patterns on the wings, the dusty wings themselves, the wings of paper, wings of shadow, and of light. The hidden grotto of beauty draws us in. And as in the old story, in the presence of these icons we might ask, "Am I the person who dreamed of being a butterfly, or the butterfly who dreamed of being human?" This is our box of dreams.

Artist's Biography

Although Dianne Kornberg was trained as a painter, her medium for twenty-five years has been photography. The subjects of her work have been specimens collected for scientific study. Most recently she has been collaborating with poets. In her work she represents the aesthetics and metaphorical ideas she finds in the natural world.

Kornberg was raised in Richland, Washington. She received her BFA from the University of Washington and her MFA from Indiana University in Painting. She is a Professor Emerita at Pacific Northwest College of Art in Portland, Oregon, and works and resides in the San Juan Islands in Washington State.

Kornberg has exhibited her work throughout the United States and internationally in more than twenty solo exhibitions. Her work is represented in several important collections including those of the Houston Museum of Art, the International Center for Photography, the Princeton Art Museum, the Portland Art Museum, the Seattle Art Museum, and the Tacoma Art Museum, and has been featured in book publications including *Contemporary Art in the Northwest*, *100 Artists of the West Coast*, and *Selected Works of the Portland Art Museum*. A monograph of her work, *Field Notes, Photographs by Dianne Kornberg, 1992–2007*, with an essay by Terry Toedtemeier, Curator of Photography at the Portland Art Museum, was published by The Art Gym, Marylhurst University, in 2007.

Artist's Statement

India Tigers

1995–2009

These butterflies and moths from India were preserved in folded, triangular paper wrappings. I photographed them so that the wrappings appear to extend out from the picture plane, as might the wing of the insect. All of the images in the series rotate on an axis around a shared, central point, and a delicate sense of movement is suggested as the direction of the light changes from one piece to the next.

This book is for Marie Churney, who has provided me with materials for my work for many years.

Publisher   Jim Leisy
Production Editor   Tom Sumner

© 2009 William, James & Company. No part of this book may be reproduced, stored in a retrieval system, transmitted, or transcribed, in any form or by any means—electronic, mechanical, telepathic, photocopy, recording, or otherwise—without prior written permission of the publisher. Requests for permission should be addressed as follows:

Rights and Permissions
William, James & Co.
22462 SW Washington Street
Sherwood, Oregon

William, James & Company is an imprint of Franklin, Beedle & Associates, Inc.

ISBN 978-1-59028-239-7

Library of Congress Cataloging-in-Publication Data is available upon request.